Yentna Old Man River

Larry Heater, Rescue Man

Yentna Old Man River

Larry Heater, Rescue Man

Lucille Heater

Northbooks
Chugiak, Alaska

Photo Credits: Personal collection of author
                Charlie, the Bear Man, p. 82–83

Poetry Credits: Maxine Clark, p. vii
                Author unknown, p. 11
                Original poetry by author, p. 16
                Author unknown, p. 19
                Kenneth Graham, p. 36
                Author unknown, p. 64
                Ma Hickle, p. 72

Published by:

ꝹORꝂꜧBOOKS

P.O. Box 671832
Chugiak, Alaska 99567
www.northbooks.com

Printed in the United States of America

ISBN 978-0-9888954-4-7

Library of Congress Control Number: 2019918426

I dedicate this book to Larry—

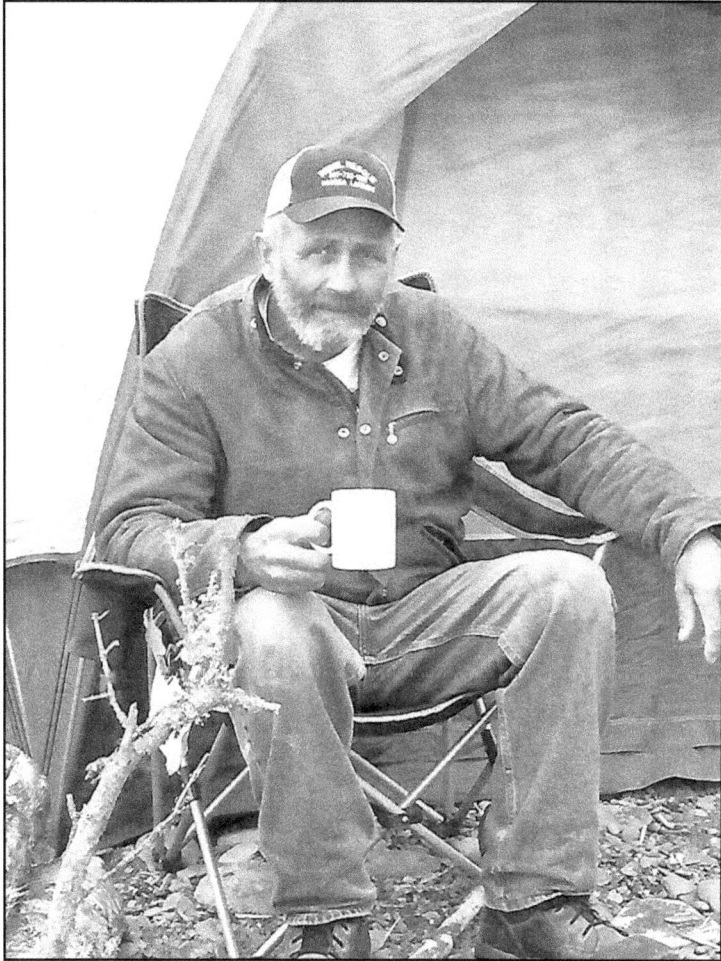

The Man

The Myth

The Legend

My Dad, Paul Monroe Heater

1897–1959

His absence is a silent grief—his life a beautiful memory.

Larry Heater

LESSONS FROM THE RIVER

Take a lesson from the river:
When obstructions try to block,
It just keeps flowing over
Or around each stone and rock.

When a mountain looms unnoticed
And is suddenly ahead,
The river meets the challenge:
Finds another course instead.

Oh the music of the river
Is a sweeter song by far,
Than if there were no obstructions
That would try its path to mar.

For the boulders add their beauty
To the foamy, rhythmic beat:
It inspires the birds to singing
And the travelers to retreat.

Can life be like a river?
Can it sing through strife and pain?
Can a person go on living
Through each sorrow, stress, and strain?

Can we find a richer channel
Round each problem hard to solve
With faith and trust in Jesus,
Walking hand in hand with God.

He can make the music sweeter
And more beautiful to sing:
And each mile growing stronger
With deeper love it brings.

For the pebbles make the music
As the river flows along,
Each obstruction adds its key note
To the music of the song.

Maxine Clark

Contents

FOREWORD

My grandpa is a River Man, not figuratively but literally. He lives, breathes, and dreams on a river in Alaska. To me, being from Missouri, Alaska has always seemed like a beautiful, magical place. My mom grew up on a mountain there, having to haul water and help cut firewood. It seems like a different world than the Ozarks. I looked forward to going to Alaska in the summers so much. The mountains, the trees, the flowers, the moose—it all felt like another world.

When I think of my grandpa, I think of a rugged, strong bearded man who could do anything. My mom and my two uncles were able to grow up under his care. Grandpa is not a person who will sugarcoat anything, but he will tell you the truth. Even if you don't want to hear it. He is tough as nails but can give a great hug that makes you feel safe.

He loved to confuse us kids with his puzzles and brainteasers. As a child, I remember sitting in total amazement that he could solve those puzzles that I could not. I looked at him with a mix of reverence and awe. He could do anything.

One of my favorite Alaskan memories is having Grandpa take me out on the river to catch salmon, and he showed me Mount Susitna, the Sleeping Lady. The story is that a young Native Alaskan woman lay down to sleep while waiting for her lover to return from battle. He died, unable to return, and she continued to sleep. She became that mountain, waiting forever.

The first time we went out on the river, I was about six years old. Grandpa had me come up to help him drive the boat and showed me Sleeping Lady. Every time we went out on the boat, I looked for Sleeping Lady. Her story has always stayed with me. It was part of the magic of Alaska. The magic my grandpa also belonged to.

Granddaughter Mary Irene Eaton
2018

Introduction

This is a book about a man who, I believe, is made of steel (not really, but I sometimes wonder).

I want to start out this book by telling you a little bit about Larry's youth.

Larry and his big brother, Dale, grew up in Clark County, Washington. They on lived on Livingston Mountain, and in those days, they could see the lights of Portland, Oregon, across the Columbia River. Over the years the trees have grown so tall that you can't see very far at all. It is beautiful country, and when Larry was growing up, it was very rural; their neighbors were far apart. Livingston Mountain is 1,935 feet in elevation and is a sister peak to Larch Mountain, which is 3,480 feet high. Larry and Dale were all over both mountains hunting deer or just hiking, loving the outdoors. Both mountains had plentiful wildlife: black bear, ruffed grouse, eagles, coyotes, bobcats, mountain lions, and, of course, deer.

Larry and Dale lived with their dad, who taught them outdoor survival from day one, sometimes in an unsympathetic way, but they both grew up wise and strong men.

Larry and Dale logged with their dad at a very young age. They also collected cascara bark. So, what is cascara bark and why did they collect it? The bark comes from cascara trees that grow in western Washington. They collected the bark to sell, and they got about thirty-five cents a pound. The bark was used to make medicine. Larry said he was told by his dad that the dry bark of cascara has been used for centuries as a laxative by the Native American Indians in the Pacific Northwest.

And now I am going to write the rest of the book in Larry's words as he told these stories to me over the years.

Lucille Heater

LARRY

Dale and I went to the dump to get our bicycle parts. We put together all the parts we had scrounged and made our first two-wheel bikes. The water source for our house was down the hill, so we changed the back sprocket on our bikes to a bigger size, so we could ride uphill easier. We would each put a five-gallon can of water on one handlebar, and then ride the bikes back up the hill. Dale and I always made it a race by yelling, "I can beat you up the hill!"

We had two flying squirrels that we caught when they were babies. They were great pets, and we had a lot of fun with them. There was neighbor lady who we called the goat woman, because she had lots of goats. The goat woman's name was Gladys, which we always called her when we visited her. We were taught to be polite. Gladys had long, black hair, even in her older years. I always said it was the goat milk that kept it so black. She was a nice lady. I remember hearing her yodel from her place over the hill to our place, several miles away. Now that woman could yodel and yodel loud. I always wondered if she was hearing her echo when she yodeled. Maybe she was calling the goats—she sure had a lot of them. So, anyway, she wanted the squirrels, and we wanted what she had—a Ford Model A pickup. And a trade was made. Even though her goats had eaten all the paint off the side of the truck, we sure got the best deal.

We ran that Model A all over those dirt roads and hills. For two country boys, we were cruising. A few years later, I had another Ford Model A pickup that I restored. I really cruised in that, then Uncle Sam found me. So, I gave it to a friend of mine.

Sometime before I was drafted, still in my teens and living on the mountain, I was on a date with this lovely girl. We came upon a deer that had been hit by a car and left in the ditch to die. We stopped, and I put the deer in the back seat of my car, and we went on. That deer got its second wind and began to make a racket; my date reached back, trying to calm the deer.

I stopped again and shot it with my .22 pistol. I took my girl home, then I went home and skinned and cut up the deer. We had some good dinners. I knew how to cook, and venison was my specialty. We ate a lot of deer.

Dad always put in a garden every spring, so we had fresh vegetables. Dale and I picked lots of blackberries during the summers. Dad made the best pie crust, and with the berries we picked, his berry pies were luscious. Dad canned up many jars of berries, vegetables, and venison every year.

We had to help in the garden, and I always had to hoe, which I hated. I'd much rather have been hunting in the woods. I decided back then that I'd never grow a garden of my own or pick up a hoe again, and I never have. Dad taught us about everything we should know in life.

One time we cut two cords of wood for a neighbor, and in turn he gave us a 1947 Indian motorcycle. My first motor-cycle, well, mine and Dale's. Little did we know it was a classic motorcycle. We did what we had to do to make it run and had fun doing it. Over the hills, gravel roads, and wherever it would go, we took turns riding, sometime riding double. Thinking back on it now, I guess we wore it out.

We cut a couple more cords of wood for the same good neighbor, and he gave us a wooden boat. It leaked, but Dad (a very wise man) patched it up with tar and canvas. We took it out on the Columbia River, where we fished for salmon and sturgeon (we could keep them if they were 40- to 60-inches long). We also fished for steelhead. I knew my dad could do just about anything. That boat did not leak, and we used it for a long time to fish to put food on our table. We ate a lot of fish. I liked fishing the Columbia River.

My brother and I used to hike up Livingston Mountain to go deer hunting, grouse hunting, or just to be outside goofing off. We would hike up to the Forest Service lookout tower, way up the mountain. Of course, we had to climb the tower and throw rocks off it, always hoping that we wouldn't get caught.

Dale, me (holding dog), and friend Mike

This is where we grew up

School Bus

The school bus did not bring us all the way home but dropped us off at a bus stop at the bottom of a hill. Dale and I had to walk the rest of the way, about two miles up this long, steep hill. Big rigs were hauling gravel, and when they came to this hill, they were going very, very slow. If we were lucky, we would be walking up this hill when the rigs came along. Why walk when we could grab the big rig's chains that were hanging in the back? We'd do just that, and let the truck pull and drag us up the hill. We let go at the wrong time so many times and then would fall flat. Finally, we learned when and where to turn loose of the chain. I wonder if that is where I started living on the edge.

Me on the left and Dale on the right. We were country boys.

Ruffed Grouse

When I was about four years old, my dad and my brother Dale and I were walking home from the town of Camas. It was about twenty-three miles to our home on Livingston Mountain, and I think we got a ride part way. Dad was carrying groceries in a gunnysack thrown over his back. I remember we had the long hill to climb up to our house. I was lagging behind them, wishing Dad would carry me.

Unknown to us, a ruffed grouse had a nest in the woods close to the road. The mama grouse heard me dragging my feet and kicking the gravel, and she came flying off her nest and hit my legs with her wings. A ruffed grouse will beat its wings against the air to create a sound that like a vacuum. She hit me so fast, flapping her wings and making that sound, that I began to run and passed Dad and Dale. I wanted to be in front of them, so I walked the rest of the way home without whining, but I kept looking back, thinking the grouse was after me.

As I grew into a young man, I learned a lot about the ruffed grouse. I learned their ways, listening to them during mating season, which is April through May. The males will drum the air with their wings, and the drumming can be heard for a long way. They start the drumroll slowly and then pick up speed, puffing out their feathers and fanning their tails. The males drum to attract the females to their territories, and once established, the males will usually remain in their territories for life. I can mimic the drumroll sound fairly well. They are pretty birds, and they are quite tasty. We never hunted them during mating season or when nesting, but in the winter we would have one or two for dinner.

BEACON ROCK

There is an 848-foot monolith on the north bank of the Columbia River, named Beacon Rock, which became a Washington State Park in 1935, two years before I was born. Dad and Dale and I climbed the rock when I was seven or eight years old, and for me, a rambunctious kid, it was a pretty good climb. We had fun on the climb. There were foot trails that zigzagged up the rock. The trail was narrow and challenging.

Beacon Rock was a landmark for boat running on the Columbia years ago; I guess when they saw the rock, they knew where they were. The Cascade Indians called the rock "Che-che-op-tin." I don't know, but maybe years ago the Indians climbed it to send smoke signals.

This is a picture of Dad, a neighbor kid named Mike, Dale, and me at the top of Beacon Rock when we hiked to the top of a mile-long switchback trail, climbing 848 feet. That's a long way to hike for little legs, but we were tough.

TOP OF BEACON ROCK

Here I am at the top of Beacon Rock in Skamania County, Washington, while on a vacation. Lucille and I drove down the Alcan to Washington to visit my cousins. The rock has changed a lot and is easy to climb now.

LUCILLE MADE IT

Lucille at the top of Beacon Rock

THE MUSIC

The Mountains are my bones
The River my veins
The forest my thoughts
And the stars are my dreams
The ocean is my heart
It's pounding in my pulse
The songs of the earth write
The music of my soul
Unknown

Just Do It

When Lucille and I started our life together, we didn't really have a plan. We did talk a lot about Alaska, though. Years ago, Dale and I saw an old trailer parked in a field with ALASKA OR BUST written in big letters. From that day on, I knew I would go to Alaska someday.

Dale was drafted into the army, and he was stationed at several different bases in and out of the USA. When the army told him that he would be stationed at Fort Richardson, Alaska, he thought that was just fine, and so he packed up his wife, Mary, and little boy, Paul, and headed up the Alcan Highway. His daughter LeeAnn was born in Alaska. Dale knew he was home.

I made a telephone call to Dale, telling him we were moving to Alaska We agreed for me to sell the old home place where we grew up. A longtime friend had always told me that if I ever wanted to sell, she would purchase it, so a deal was made. I sent Dale his half, and I knew where I was going with the other half. I had been driving a dump truck for Thompson Trucking; I gave the owner the keys and said to him, "Alaska, here I come."

We packed our pickup and camper and pulled a trailer. The trailer was stacked and crammed with what we thought we might need. My rifles, as I knew I would need a rifle for hunting moose. A freezer stuffed full of household goods and other things. An old trunk that we filled with stuff. Cast-iron pans, one of my grandma's crocks, Lucille had one of her grandma's crocks, and a crock bowl that Dad made sourdough pancakes in every morning for as long as I can remember, and an antique whiskey jug. We packed pictures and lots of Lucille's books. We also packed several spare tires, warm clothing, and boots for six people: Lucille, four kids, and me. Dog food for three dogs (one gave birth to five puppies equals eight). Lots of oatmeal and beef stew, water, plus other food that would be easy to fix. We ate a lot of oatmeal and beef stew on our trip.

The trip went pretty well until the Alcan began to get slick with ice. I figured I would stop and put chains and snow tires on when I thought it wasn't going to get any better.

The colder it got, the old Ford pickup's windows and windshield began to ice up, because the truck's defroster was not working very well. I told Lucille to get the can of defroster. She couldn't open the top, so I said, "Give it to me." I gave it a twist, and I guess I turned the steering wheel. The truck swerved, hit a snow berm, slid right into a snow-filled ditch, and came to a sudden stop. The truck was tilting, and, of course, the camper was tilted, so it woke up the kids while clothing and stuff fell out of the cabinets. No one was hurt. I got out and checked the radiator and truck—nothing damaged.

Now to get out of the ditch. A Jeep came along and tried to pull us out, but the truck didn't budge. A tour bus stopped and tried to pull us out, but the bus started sliding sideways, and our truck didn't move. I started digging with a shovel, then a semi-truck stopped; he had his truck all chained up. The trucker hooked a chain to our truck and with one pull, out it came. We all pulled over on the road and Lucille made coffee and cocoa, and I invited the trucker to eat breakfast with us, as we did have fixings for that. No oatmeal that morning. I thanked the driver, and he went on south, and we headed on north. I would bet the driver was thinking, "Darn cheechakos!"

We went on for a few more miles when I slid all the way down a huge hill. I then decided I should put on our chains. The boys helped put the chains on, Lucille made some more coffee and cocoa, we got all warmed up again and went on our way. Each kid took turns riding up in front with Lucille and me.

Rest stop—checking my trailer load.
Lucille packed everything but the kitchen sink.

Alaska or Bust

We made it to Alaska almost bust. We had five hundred dollars left to find a place to live and for groceries. First thing, I signed up for unemployment. The ink was barely dry before I got a call to check on a job. We were ready to get on our way to Seward for a week of fun. I went to see what the job was about and was hired to start the next day. There went our trip to Seward. I worked for ABC Towing and Wrecking's owners, Rodney and Sheila Lewis, for thirteen years.

ABC Towing and Wrecking

MY MAN

My man, darn old junk-yard man,
He leaves home just before the break of light
Comes home dog-tired at night

He is grease and grime up past his chin
But he always comes in with a big, big grin

He grabs me around to kiss me Hi
Leaves a mark of grease above my eye

But I wouldn't trade my junk-yard man, for all
the lily-white hands in the land

He smashes them old junk-yard cars
with the crusher to and fro
And up to his ass in this Alaskan snow

He always comes home, happy as can be
That's perfect happiness
Because he is coming home to me.

                                        Lucille Heater

First Sand Bar

Things have really changed since I made my first cheechako trip down the Big Susitna River. We launched my boat at the Susitna Landing at Mile 82.5 off the Parks Highway on the Kahiltna River and were ready to go. Right out of the Susitna Landing, the Kahiltna splits in two before it runs into the Susitna River. I saw a big boat go to the right and thought this must be the way out to the Susitna River, so I thought, "I'll just go out to the right." I did, and I hit a sand bar and stopped abruptly, still within sight of the landing. We got out of the boat and started pushing to get back into deeper water. I told Lucille to not let go of the boat, as we might step in deep water a few feet farther. We got the boat floating, and we got back into the boat. That was my first lesson: Don't just follow someone—think things through and use my own judgement. The guy we followed had a jet, and we had a prop.

I knew I had to learn to read this river quickly and to remember the landmarks. As we went on down the river, it soon turned into fingers, which means the river flows into five different channels. I was thinking about which one to take. I chose the wrong one, and we came upon a huge log jam and had to turn around. Now this was interesting: having to turn around in swift-flowing, silty water that is hitting the logs that are bouncing up and down as if to say, "I'm gonna get you!"

I knew this would not have a happy ending if the motor stalled. The log jam would take the boat, Lucille, and me right under. I managed to get the boat turned around, and I didn't look back. I took another channel that took us on downriver. When I looked at Lucille, she was in panic mode. I didn't say much to her until she calmed down later when we got to the Deshka River.

YOUNGSTOWN BEND

I boated out of Susitna Landing on our first trip to Youngstown Bend by boat. We had flown in a few times before, but this time we were headed ninety miles up the Yentna River to explore and play on our newly purchased five acres.

We were using lots of gas, so I had to stop along the way to refuel the boat. As I look at the photo that we took that day, I think we were a little overloaded.

We found that the river was smooth and straight at times, and other times it was winding. I had many surprises on this trip and some thrills, and sometimes Lucille was terrified. I got us to our destination, though, with more river lessons learned.

We enjoyed our week up there, and the next trip up there by boat was enjoyable. It was a beautiful river trip. When it was a sunny day, we could play hide and seek with Denali on many turns of the river.

It took so much time to get up to the property for just a weekend, I began to wonder if this property was the right place for us. We were both working in town and really did not have time to enjoy the land because of the time it took to get up there. Unless I bought an airplane. I was taking flying lessons, so maybe that would be a possibility. In the meantime, though, I told Lucille to keep looking for a place on the lower Yentna.

OLD CABIN

Keep your heart open for dreams,
For as long as there's a dream,
There is hope, and as long as there is hope,
There is joy in living.

Unknown

We spent our weekends looking for property along the lower Yentna River. We had passed this one place with an old cabin several times, wishing it had a for-sale sign. One weekend I told Lucille, "I am going to stop at this old cabin. It looks as if someone is there." I stopped, and we went up to talk to the folks. As we were getting ready to leave after visiting, I said to them, "If you ever want to sell, here is my phone number. I am very interested in your place." We left, thinking that it had been just a visit and that we'd made some new friends.

A couple of years later, the couple called and said they wanted to sell. We knew we wanted the place, so we talked and made the deal. It seemed like a good deal to us. It had a cabin on it and a freshwater spring that never freezes in the winter, with the best-tasting water. I then told Lucille, "Here is your cabin in the woods."

We spent a lot of weekends in this cabin, and then begin to think of more space. We did eventually build on to the old cabin and decided to open a winter lodge. Soon we had people stopping by for coffee and hamburgers. We called the lodge Rebel Roost, which turned out to be a great business. As the years went by, we made many wonderful memories of meeting Alaskans and lots of others that vacationed from the Lower 48 and foreign countries. We have wonderful river friends. During the summers, our grown children and grandchildren visited us often, helping cut wood and going fishing.

Big Swirls in River

One summer Amie, our first granddaughter, came out to stay awhile with us. She loved to fish, and even at her young age, she baited her own hooks and her grandma's. Since Lucille did not drive a boat, I took Amie and her down to a slough that wasn't too far from the lodge. I towed my little boat that had a small motor, and they got into the small boat. I anchored it in the slough and went back to the lodge to work.

Amie and Lucille fished and fished, and when they got their limit, they watched a bear playing and fishing at the other end of the slough, wondering if Grandpa had forgotten them.

A while later I went down and pulled into the slough. Lucille stood up to pull up the anchor in the little boat and called out that she couldn't get in my boat unless I came closer. I told her I wasn't coming over closer, that she was going to drive the little boat back to the lodge.

Amie's eyes got real big, and Lucille didn't look very happy about it. I could tell she was getting mad and was thinking some nasty words.

I started yelling instructions, telling her how to start the motor. She got it started but didn't know how to use the tiller. I was yelling more instructions, and she was yelling, "I don't want to do this! Amie is in the boat with me." I told her, "Well, sit here all night or drive the boat." She told me she would be sitting there all night.

I turned my boat around and took off fast, went a little way, and then slowed down to see if she got out of the slough. Lucille slowly gave the little boat some gas and did get out of the slough into the wide river. She gave the boat some more gas and was running along pretty well. When they almost got to the lodge, she ran across one of those big swirls that I had seen in the river many times. She gripped the handle, but that swirl knocked the tiller right out of her hand. The boat jumped, the motor slowed, and Amie fell flat onto the bottom of the boat. Lucille grabbed the tiller again and gave the boat some more gas—a little too much. She hit the riverbank at the lodge with half the boat ending up on the bank.

She got out of that boat and gave me some choice words. "Was this any way to teach your wife how to drive a boat? I'll never drive a boat again!" And she never did.

Here I am teaching Amie to drive a boat some years later

Moose Creek

Lucille wrote this story about our friends before they passed. She told Elaine that she would put it in a book someday. When Elaine passed, Lucille read it at Elaine's celebration of life, and I'm including it here in memory of Elaine and Ray.

WONDERFUL MEMORIES OF FRIENDS WE WILL ALWAYS REMEMBER

ELAINE 1942–2014   RAY 1943–2017

ELAINE ALWAYS SAID, "DON'T WORRY ABOUT TOMORROW, GOD'S ALREADY THERE."

Ray and Elaine were great neighbors and became our good friends. They are lucky they found the Moose Creek property before we did. Before we bought the property on the lower Yentna, I was still looking over maps and acreage to buy. I spotted some acreage on Moose Creek, and I looked up the information to see if it could be purchased from the state. It had already been taken. I didn't give up, so I went digging and found out the owner was Ray M. I proceeded to give the man a call at his office and asked him if he was interested in selling. He gave me a definite no. He said it had a small cabin on it, and it was to be his retirement home. Okay, I gave that idea up quickly.

Larry and I had fished Moose Creek for a couple of summers prior to my conversation. Later after talking with him, when we fished up the creek, we would gawk at the little cabin and say, "No wonder he didn't want to sell. It is such a peaceful setting, and the only cabin on the creek."

As it turned out, the property that we eventually bought on the lower Yentna wasn't too far from Ray and Elaine's place on Moose Creek, so they were our Moose Creek neighbors.

Elaine was from down South in Mississippi. She is a happy lady with Southern hospitality. She can whip up an elegant meal and serve it with the Southern charm of a true, classy Alaskan lady, which she had become. You don't go away hungry from her table. Ray is a true sourdough: long beard and cob pipe (seldom lit) in his mouth. He's always ready to tell a good joke or a story about his great retirement life at Moose Creek. Ray always teased me about trying to buy his place. He seldom goes to town; in fact, it's been about three years now since he has seen the city lights. When he was close to retirement, he knew he was going to take down his shingle and didn't care if he would ever see the city lights again.

They have a special sitting deck where they can sit and feel the summer breeze and watch the wildlife that happens by. During the winter, while sitting by a warm fire, they look out a large window to watch the wildlife show. A grizzly ambles out of the woods through their yard. The bear is huge, and if there were any danger, that bear could stand his ground. The Moose Creek bear are no danger on this creek, as Ray and Elaine sit quietly to watch and observe the greatness of this beautiful creature.

Black bears play along the creek banks; the cubs put on a show, climbing up the trees and back down, wrestling, rolling around, and sometimes getting a little physical with each other. They need those activities to develop skills to survive. Cubs learn to climb at an early age. Their mother will send them up a tree while she feeds, or if danger is near.

Elaine told us that while sitting on the deck, she watched an eagle as it dived down on two beautiful white swans. The big swan flapped its wings and knocked the eagle head over heels. The eagle went and sat on a log for the longest time. You wonder what was going through its mind after the swan had taken the wind out of his sail. After the eagle rested, he flew over and picked a salmon out of the creek.

A peregrine falcon is also an extremely powerful flyer. It is one of the fastest flying birds in the world. It can reach speeds up to nearly 200 miles per hour while diving. Elaine has seen a falcon plunge down and pick a mallard duck right out of the creek. Occasionally a grey hawk plucks a duck out of the creek for its lunch.

Ray told us that one night when he was outside, he turned his flashlight on and saw two huge yellow eyes staring back at him. It was a large black wolf. It was Ray's birthday, so he told the large wolf it was his lucky night. I'm not sure who was the lucky one.

On Moose Creek there is an old trapper cabin sitting on a little rise before you get to Ray's place. We used to stop and go up to the cabin. We were told a man named Cliff had built and used it for many years. I would guess he was trapping; it would have been a good location back in the old days, long before statehood. It was incredible to just stand and look at the structure. You go back into the past in your mind, and you start to feel so envious. You know you were born in the wrong century, and how interesting it must have been to roam and build a tiny cabin and trap with no one around but yourself and nature. I think Ray and Elaine experience a bit of that past by living up Moose Creek with no one living close by. They see an abundance of wildlife and have so many wonderful stories to tell. Ray could be a one-man act, sitting on a stage telling his stories. You can visualize what he is saying, he tells them so well. He gives a story life and laughter.

Ray and Elaine are two blessed friends. When you leave their home, you always have a smile on your face and a piece of dessert in your pocket.

Through the years that we have known them, they have either been building onto or remodeling their log home. Elaine had a vision, and with Ray's knowledge, they built the most unique and beautiful log home built in the bush, They designed the house to utilize the local forest resources, using lots of spruce burls and making amazing and creative things from them. A lot of the burls were peeled, and that's not an easy job.

A burl is a growth on a spruce tree in which the grain has grown in a deformed manner on the side of the tree, forming different patterns. Ray and Elaine both went into the woods together to search for the burls they liked. I believe they found every pattern imaginable. Their home is difficult to describe in words that will do it justice. Each piece, every log was a vision, and they made it into reality.

One time they found a large tree that had a huge burl and that could be carved out easily. They placed it in the bathroom. The burl had a big hole in it and made a perfect fit to go over the honey bucket. Ray then carved a lid for it to place on top of the burl over the honey bucket. No more night runs for the outhouse, and it was a beautiful piece. They made lots of things: chairs, tables, stairs with burls—anything imaginable. Whenever you went inside the house, everything was neatly in place.

They made a cellar under the house that you entered from inside the house. Ray made an insulated wooden box. He had a buddy help him set it down in the hole he had dug for it. Ray had scribed the hole and the box slid right in the hole perfectly. That is a true story.

On one evening when Larry and I were up visiting Ray and Elaine, Ray and Larry went out on the frozen pond across the frozen creek. They jumped up and down on the ice, taking turns. While one would jump, the other would light the gas that spurted up. They were laughing like crazy. Elaine and I were sitting on the deck, watching and laughing with them. The two men we love are still like little boys. We always enjoyed our visits with them.

Elaine, Ray, Lucille, and Larry

YENTNA STATION

The Yentna Station is a wonderful lodge to stop in to eat and visit for a while. Dan and Jennie raised their six kids at the Yentna Station. The kids are now grown-up and are entrepreneurs, married, and raising families of their own. We have been friends with Dan and Jennie since 1979 or 1980. They host the Junior Iditarod Dog Races and the great Iditarod Races to Nome.

Something that I remember is that one time, Dan hosted Ted Turner (yes, the real Ted Turner) and a few of his employees for a fishing party. Lucille and I came out to help.

I took a few guys and gals up to Kutna slough. It is a great place to catch some nice fish. I told the ladies to be careful because the mud along the banks is very slick and gooey. One lady just got out of the boat, slipped on the mud, and fell flat, face forward. Her hands were under the mud and only her long pink fingernails were sticking out. Her co-workers were laughing, and the lady said, "Well, if you think it's so funny, take a picture." They did, of course, and it was a funny story to tell when they got back from fishing. They had pictures to back up their stories.

If a person didn't want to fish, there were other things to stretch the truth about. There was volleyball to play or good music to listen to. Dan plays a mean twelve-string guitar, and along with other aspiring musicians playing their instruments, they made very good music. A lovely lady, Candy, who lived upriver, joined in singing, and she had beautiful voice.

When it was time for Mr. Turner to leave, the float plane came in as close to the shore as it could, so that Ted wouldn't get his feet wet. The plane had to be pushed away from the bank to taxi for takeoff, so I handed Mr. Turner my boat paddle to use to push out.

He could have easily thrown it back to me; instead, Turner just threw the paddle in the river, and off the airplane goes. And off down the river my boat paddle goes. I was pissed. Of course, I will never see Ted Turner again. But if I do, I will remind him he owes me a boat paddle.

I am looking for you, Ted Turner!

REBEL ROOST TOWING
AND RESCUE

I enjoyed the lodge business, but after a few more years and a heart problem, I decided we should begin another trail in our life. When we sold the Rebel Roost, we knew our hard work had paid off, and that's when we moved to the Deshka subdivision. Through the years I always liked to use the Deshka Landing, in fact I think I was the first boat to use it when Earle and Rhea Foster opened the Landing, and I continued to use it.

Now I own Rebel Roost Towing and Rescue, a towing and barge business. I am on the river almost every day. I enjoy hauling building supplies, fuel for friends, picking up floaters, and going out on river rescues.

I tell Lucille that I call the river my church. I see the beauty of God's creations every day. I come home telling Lucille about seeing eagles sitting in the trees close to the riverbank when the salmon come upriver. At times I will see a bear swimming across the river. I also see moose swimming in the river to get away from the agonizing mosquitoes.

I always wondered how the salmon knew to leave the ocean and return to the same freshwater streams. Lucille said most salmon will return to the precise spot of their birthplace, where they will spawn, and then die. It's been that homing behavior in salmon that depends on an olfactory memory of smell and the recollection of odors. I learned something, and now I just think how very smart salmon are.

Smoking Fish

It was a great year for salmon. I had my smokehouse filled, and I had my alder cut, so that I could keep the smokehouse smoking. Buck and I were sitting in the house, talking about anything and everything. I heard a snap, and I knew it was my smokehouse latch. I looked out, and a big black bear had the smoker door open. The bear was just standing there, looking in and trying to decide where to start on his smorgasbord.

I ran outside, yelling profanity at him. I grabbed up a two by four and ran toward the bear, swinging that board. The bear looked at me, and then looked back to the smoked fish, then looked at me again. I guess he knew I meant business, so off he ran.

I then checked the smoker to see if my fish was finished, it was not, so I knew I would have to keep a better watch on it, as I figured the bear would be back.

Buck and I retreated to the deck to have a better view. Buck looked at me and said, "I can't believe what you just did—a two by four?" I told him that bear was not going to get my fish.

The bear never returned, and the fish got smoked. I figured the bear thought I was a madman, yelling and swinging that two by four.

THE INEBRIATED RABBIT

Lucille's sister, Joy, my sister-out-law (as I liked to tease her) had flown in from California to visit us at the Deshka Landing. Billy and I had gone rabbit hunting, and I had two nice rabbits to cook for dinner. I had to clean and soak them until it was time to cook. The recipe is that you roll the rabbit pieces in flour that has salt and pepper in it, heat oil in a skillet, and place the pieces in the hot oil. When they are brown on one side, flip them over to brown the other side, then you usually put in one quarter cup of water to steam for a few minutes.

Joy had brought a bottle of California wine to have with dinner, and the wine got opened before dinner. She served me a small glass of wine while I was cooking, and I tasted it but didn't like the taste. Joy was talking and not watching, so I poured the wine in with the cooking rabbit. Joy poured me another small glass of wine, thinking I had finished the first glass. She left the room, and I poured the wine in the skillet with the rabbit. Joy returned and gave me another small glass of wine. I sipped on it, and Joy left the room again. That wine went into the rabbit too, which by now was really steaming. A total of about three quarters of a cup of wine made that rabbit turn out very tender and luscious.

Joy pulled out another bottle of wine for dinner. But I told her that I'd had enough wine, and that I would switch to my Wild Turkey.

BOAT SINKING

The river keeps calling "Old Man River," a name that Ms. Payton gave me. It just kind of took off from that. When I need to load my barge, I have a loader that I use. With it I can load barrels of fuel, lumber, or equipment by myself. I have been doing it for so many years, I can tell about when the boat is loaded right. When I put freight in the barge, I have a mark on the side of the boat that I use, so that I know if I'm level and not overloaded.

One day I was hauling fuel for one of the fish camps along the river for Fish and Game. Passing the Deshka River, which runs into the Susitna, I kept looking at the water in my boat—the pump wasn't pumping fast enough. Looking a little closer, I saw water flowing in fast. I assumed I had gotten a hole in the hull somehow.

I decided to turn around, and I called Lucille to ask Andy (one of our friends) to get my boat trailer and back it up deep into the water at the launch. I told her that I didn't know if I would make it back to the landing, and that I thought the barge was very close to sinking. I told her that I had put on my life jacket, so she knew I had a real concern.

It took a while, but I made it back upriver, and as I came around the bend, I saw Lucille and Andy waiting for me at the landing. I had a boat full of water and fuel. We brought the boat back to the house, then I reloaded my tow boat with the fuel, and took it on down to the fish camp.

My barge did have a hole in it that I had to get welded up, because the barge is the boat that hauls big loads. I found out that I had a tire on the trailer that had eventually rubbed a hole into the side about the size of a silver dollar. Got it fixed and was soon on the river again.

Went to Sleep

It was a nice summer day; the weather was hot, and the sun was shining through my boat windshield. I'd had a rescue at 2 a.m., helping a boater out of a distressing situation, so I was tired and sleepy. My boat was running just fine, and then I came to a sudden stop. My head hit the windshield, and that's what woke me up. Yep, I had fallen asleep, and my boat was up on the bank of the Susitna River. I was sitting there contemplating my awful situation and rubbing my head when I heard a boat coming upriver.

They stopped and asked if I was having trouble. I said in a joking way, "I can get my boat started, but it won't move."

"Well, you need it in the water to move," the lady said.

After a brief conversation, I asked for a ride to the Deshka Landing, and they agreed to take me there. I got Ron, my neighbor, to take his boat down to help get my boat off the bank. We started out by breaking the first rope, and then realized that my boat wasn't going to come off the bank so easy. I had landed on a mud bank that was as sticky as glue.

We jacked the front end of the boat up and put a log under it, then Ron got back in his boat, pulled again, and my boat came loose. I went on home, thinking that was enough for one day.

This is what happens when you don't get enough sleep

Foggy

At times when I leave the Deshka Landing, the sky is blue, and I think it's going to be a nice river run. Then when I get downriver, the fog looks like a wall. I go ahead and motor into it, thinking the fog will lift. I keep going but a little slower. If it gets where I can't see at all, I will stop and wait it out.

My windshield was broken when I fell asleep and put the boat on the riverbank and my head banged into the windshield. I motor on a mile or so and out pops Sleeping Lady. I had made it through the fog, and now my trip is nice and sunny. When I got down to what is called Seal Island on the Susitna, by the mouth of the Yentna, there are several seals on the island. The seals follow the hooligan, which are a type of smelt that are going up the rivers and streams to spawn, and the hooligan runs are on both sides of the river. The small fish are an important forage species for eagles, bears, gulls, and seals.

I see so many wonderful things when I am on the river, and that fresh air feels great, too.

My windshield that was broken when I fell asleep
and put my boat on the riverbank

THE RIVER IS MY WORLD

The River, it's my world, and I don't want any other,
What it hasn't got is not worth having,
And what it doesn't know, it's not worth knowing.
Lord, the times we've had together.

Kenneth Graham

Summer Floaters

In the summers when the fish are finding their way up the Susitna and Yentna Rivers and the many tributaries to lay their eggs, many people come up to float the streams. They come to fish, to watch for bear, to camp out, or to just relax on their float trips. I often take folks up to Moose Creek, off Petersville Road, for their float trips.

They start at mile 104 of the Parks Highway. It usually takes at least a week or longer to do the float trip from that point at Moose Creek. Sometimes I will go up to Petersville with them and drive their truck back to the landing. Then after the float, I will pick them up at the Deshka River and bring them here to the Deshka Landing.

GOING WITH THE FLOW

I picked up these guys at the Deshka River. They had floated down from Moose Creek, off Petersville Road. They said they had a good float and caught fish to cook after they set up their camp each evening.

Memories are made going with the flow

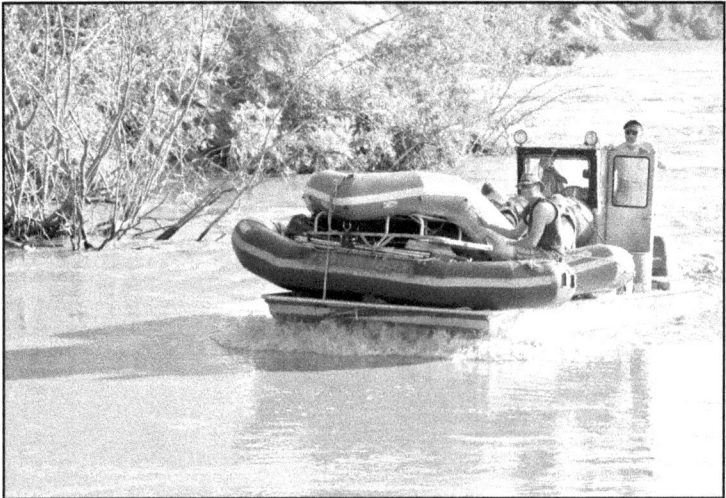

Fourteen Men Floating

This had to be a great float trip. There were four rafts, fourteen guys, and supplies for the two-week float. They put their rafts in at Moose Creek off Petersville Road, and they floated. Just imagine seeing all the natural beauty along that float trip.

When they reached the mouth of the Deshka River, I picked up the party with my barge and brought them to the Deshka Landing. They had a terrific time on their float. This was a happy bunch of guys who were all smiles. I sure enjoyed them.

GREAT FLOAT TRIPS

Friendship is a good thing. To go floating and camping and to make so many good memories with friends is even better. Having summer fun, fishing, and watching for wildlife while slowly floating the rivers. Camping in the evenings, looking at the stars, telling stories on each other, belly laughing, and drinking good coffee. What a wonderful summer vacation.

Good friends are like the stars, you don't always see them, but you know they are always there. This was a great float trip.

Picking up some other floaters at the mouth of the Deshka River. These guys and gals had floated from Moose Creek to the mouth of the Deshka. They said they had enjoyed the trip fishing and camping.

It's a wonderful way to enjoy family and friends.

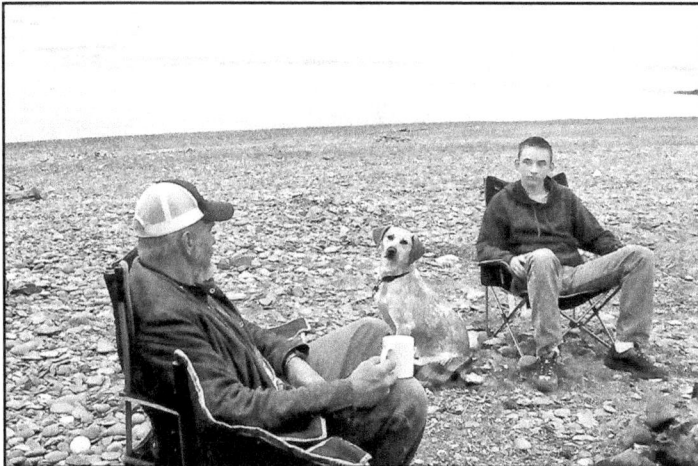

I did take time off to enjoy my family.
With grandson Billy Jr., sharing words of wisdom.

LITTLE MOOSE RESCUE

I rescued this little moose off the river where he had fallen on the ice. The little guy didn't try to hurt me when I put him in my sled; I think he was too scared. I brought him to my yard where I hoped to save him. I winched him up to stand, and that's when I noticed his leg was broken. He could not stand by himself. I felt so sorry for him, as he was in good health otherwise. I called the Alaska Fish and Game, hoping they would take him to a rescue place. I was told to take him to a patch of willows, where he could eat and heal. I did that, telling the little guy good luck. But in my heart, I didn't think he would make it.

MY MOST INTERESTING RESCUE

You need to visualize this rescue. Notice the steering wheel. This is the funniest rescue I ever did. When I told Lucille about it, I could couldn't stop laughing.

A good friend of ours got in their van, and the seat was pushed all the way forward. She scooted onto the seat, barely getting her body in. When she did get in, her boobs fell into the two holes in the steering wheel. One boob in one side and the other in the second opening, and they got lodged. She tried to pull them out, and then tried to scoot the seat back. Nothing would budge. She had the van running, so she thought of the me, the rescue man.

She drove over from their parking space, which is on the overflow parking lot to our house. She was slumped over, with her boobs stuck in the steering wheel and her body wedged in the seat. She could barely see through the windshield, but she managed to drive. I was outside the house when she got there. I walked over to the van and said, "You having some trouble?"

"I think so," she said, and explained what had happened.

I observed the situation and pushed the seat back. Unfortunately, that stretched her boobs a little more, but she didn't complain. I gently helped to get them dislodged. I could hardly contain my laughter but did the rescue and told her there would be no charge for the rescue.

She replied, "I should charge you!"

By then we were both laughing. She went on to town, and I went in the house and told Lucille, "I just did the funniest rescue, and I wish I'd had a video camera. We would be rich from that TV show, *America's Funniest Home Videos*."

No names have been used, except Lucille's and mine. Sorry, my friend, I just had to write about all my rescues, and I just could not leave this one out.

FIRE

At daybreak I got a call from a guy for a rescue. He was planning to go moose hunting. He told me that he had come out the night before and camped. He checked his camp gear and secured his boat before walking around the island to check out moose sign. He had planned to make his camp for a few days' stay.

He walked to the backside of the island and saw some promising moose signs. The weather was cool, the leaves were in their fall colors, so he was going to go back to fix up his camp, rest a while, and go back out in the evening hours.

Before he could start back to camp, he heard a very loud KABOOM and lots of popping sounds. He hurried to get back around the end of the island, and then he saw flames. He had lots of gas in his boat and the rest of his camping supplies. The boat was burning fast and hot. There was no way he could save it. All he could do now was to call for a rescue. And that's who called me at daybreak.

BROKEN-DOWN BOAT

Sometimes a planned weekend does not go the way you planned. I'm sure the kids were excited and then disappointed, when the boat broke down. Their dad had to call for a Rebel Rescue. I piled them all in my tow boat and made sure all the kids had life jackets on. I hooked up the broken-down boat and upriver we came to take them back safely to the Deshka Landing. I'm sure the dad was wondering what could be wrong with his boat. It turned out to be a different boat trip than they'd planned. Things happen for a reason.

TREES AND FUEL

This boatload of trees is going up to my friend Jim's. Jim and Nancy built a hexagon house, and they did a fantastic job building it. They were landscaping and decided they needed more trees.

On another day, I'm hauling fuel. This is going up the Yentna.

Rescue

Another rescue for me, Old Man River. Towing a broken-down boat with 3,000 pounds of lumber on it. A bad day for him—a good day for me.

River Hauls

When Lucille and I were going through the photos of all my freight hauls, we realized how many I've done over the years. We've only included about a third of them in this book.

This Jeep went to Jones on the upper Yentna River

This pickup truck was the first pickup I loaded on my boat and hauled. It went up to Webber at Webber's Slough on the lower Yentna.

FISH WHEELS

A load of fish wheels going out to the guys and gals on the Yentna. They will set them up and count fish and perform other duties for the summer. Most of the crew are college students, working summer jobs for Fish and Game. They are a nice and intelligent young group.

During the summer, Fish and Game hires me to haul fuel, along with delivering fish wheels up and down the river. They also have me move the fish wheels from one location to another. I've done this for a few years. I am always impressed with the young men and women who work for Fish and Game on the river. They all seem to work together to get the jobs done by the end of summer.

Here, at the Main Stem Camp, the team is getting ready to take the fish wheels down to be loaded on the boat, and then I will haul them back to the Deshka Landing.

This load of fuel is going to the Flat Horn Camp

LOADING UP

Just another beautiful day on the river

Imm's Inn

These two loads and many more went up the Yentna River to the Imm's when they were building their lodge, Imm's Inn. They are open for business year-round.

Larry Imm, owner of Imm's Inn

HAULING FREIGHT

Down the Susitna River and up the Yentna River.

ON TIPTOE

This was an interesting haul to Mile 9 on the Yentna River. I had stand on tiptoe in order to see the river. I knew the landmarks, so it was a fairly easy trip, but next day my neck and toes sure were sore.

Another day, another dollar. I love my job.

HEWITT LAKE

I have always enjoyed going to Hewitt Lake, but getting into the lake can sometimes be tricky. I need to be careful because of logs, leaning trees, and brush along the channel. I don't like to tear up props. Once I'm past all that, though, I enter the lake. On this day I was delivering fuel to the lodge. I enjoy their friendship and the lunch they always have ready for me.

METAL STEPS

These metal steps were going to Hewitt Lake, I had already hauled up 46,000 pounds of lumber, as my friend was building a house on a hill. In the first photo, I was leaning against my boat, trying to figure out how to load the steps. I had to make sure that when I got them loaded that my boat would be as level as possible. I decided to take the steps up in two loads, two sections per trip.

Loading the steps onto the boat was easy with my loader, but getting each section off the boat would be challenge. At the lake it was all manpower. We winched and roped and pushed and pulled. Even with three guys, it was not an easy job, but by working together we got it done and up the hill.

MORE HAULS AND TWO BIRDS

MY HOBBY

My barge is my hobby and my retirement. I would never want to do anything else in my leisure time for fun. I will be on the river every chance I get. The river is a challenge to me in the sunshine, snow, fog, ice, rain, or wind. Bring it on. I only challenge myself.

My other hobby

Airboat

I did a little hauling in my airboat. I really liked using it, but a guy from Canada made me an offer I could not refuse. The boat is somewhere on the Yukon.

Giving my neighbor a ride down the Big Su River in my second airboat

Just Floating Down a River

A smile on the face is a sign that the heart is at home.
Unknown

MIKE AND MERT'S DESHKA RIVER LODGE

When I took this load and went up to Mike and Mert's, I had to look through the cabin's side window to see the river. I didn't mind, since I was only going to the mouth of the Deshka River. I got it there, and Mike had to get it up the high bank to his lodge. Mike used his loader, but it was still tricky working on the riverbank and getting the load out of my barge. We did it, though, and Mike took it up the high bank to the lodge. Everything falls in place—if you're patient.

SAD DAY

This was a very sad day in May on the Deshka River. Two airboats collided as they rounded a river curve. The outcome was not good; two people were killed. It was a depressing load when I hauled one of the boats back to the Deshka Landing.

DOING MY JOB

Every day may not be good, but there is something good in every day. These days are good days. I'm in my boat doing what I love.

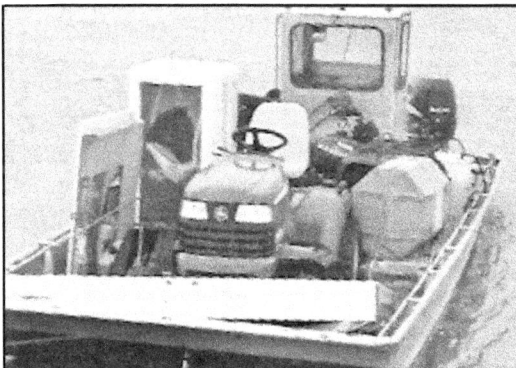

WINTER RIDING

When the river freezes up, it's time for riding snowmachines. A person gets a lot of enjoyment meeting up with friends out in the fresh air. Some folks travel on the Deshka, Susitna, or Yentna Rivers after they freeze up. They go to their cabins hauling in supplies to build or repair a sauna or to add on a deck, or maybe to work on an outhouse. Others just ride to go to a lodge for a hamburger and beer. Whatever the reason might be, they are out enjoying time with their families and friends.

I am the Rebel Rescue Old Man River during the winter, as well as in the summer. I tow broken-down snowmachines, and I rescue snowmachincs that fall through the ice when the riders don't watch where they are going. I haul supplies, lumber, and fuel among other things.

I enjoy my winters when I am on my frozen river.

EACH WINTER

Each winter in Alaska is different. There is either no snow, too much snow, just the right amount of snow, overflow, hard ice, soft ice, great trails, no trails, cold temperatures, warm temperatures. You name it, Alaska can give it to you. It is a beautiful state, but the winters can be brutal. Or the winters can be perfect.

Each year new cabins are built along these rivers. Usually a guy will build a shop first on his newly purchased land. Why? Because he can put his tools and chain saw and stuff inside to keep the bears from scattering things. All his tools will all be safe and handy when he builds his cabin.

This is a 1956 Artic Cat I bought one year, thinking it would be great to make a trail. I drove this cat all the way to Yentna Station from the end of Knik Road. It was not easy to drive, and it was slow, a real snail crawl. I could have outrun the machine. It did make a heck of a nice trail, though. Lucille followed me on her snowmachine, and she said it was no fun going so slow. I got that Cat back home and never drove it again. I sold it.

A real leader faces the music even though he doesn't like the tune.
Anonymous

River Experiences

Traveling on the river in winter can be dangerous, especially when snowmachines go through the ice. That's when Rebel Rescue is called out again. I don't always have the answers; some ideas work, and some don't. We finally managed to pull all these snowmachines out of the water or the ice holes they had fallen into.

SCARY TREE

Scary Tree was always a pit stop in the winter when riding snowmachines. Anyone who rode a snowmachine knew about the Scary Tree stop. It was a place to take out the coffee or open a beer or have a sip of whiskey.

Ma Hickle and friends stopped by the tree one evening. She looked up at the tree and said, "Dang, that's a scary tree!" From that time on, it was called Scary Tree. She wrote a poem about it, which I have included. The tree has fallen, but for twenty years it was thc Scary Tree stop.

A beacon in the night
Lets us know our trail is right
A place for friends to meet
Passersby we greet
On this corner at your feet

Even though you no longer stand
This place, to me,
Will always be

Scary Tree
Ma Hickle

GET THE SHOVEL

Anything can happen when riding a snowmachine on the rivers or ice trails. There can be overflow somewhere on the river. I try to plan when I should leave home. How is the weather? What's the forecast for the day? Has it snowed like crazy miles from here? Is there any wind? Has it been blowing, perhaps covering an overflow?

My trip for the day was a long one; I was headed for Hewitt Lake. It wasn't my day to get stuck, but it was for a couple of other snowmachines with sleds. It was time for them to get their shovels out and dig. Others stop by to see if they can help. I always offer to help, but the guys usually have it under control.

ALPINE I

I started out with an Alpine snowmachine. It's a great machine that would pull heavy loads and would seldom leave me stranded. But it would occasionally get stuck if the snow wasn't the right condition—if the trail was soft or if there was an overflow. Lucille used to help me haul a few loads, and if there was an overflow in the trail, I would go through first. She would hesitate, and I would have to yell and tell her to hit the gas and come through fast. She would do just that and keep on going, then she would stop and wait for me.

One night we were coming back to the Deshka Landing from a freight run when I hit an overflow. Lucille was behind me on another machine and stopped. She walked up to where I knew it was slush, but I didn't know how deep the overflow was. I was on the machine and putting the gas to it. Lucille was pushing from behind, and very quickly she was up to her thighs in slush. She stepped over a bit and onto ice, so I hit the gas again as she was pushing. The darn machine came out of the slush very quickly with Lucille holding on. When I looked back, I was dragging her. She said she was afraid to let go. She walked back to her machine and went maybe three feet to the left of the deep hole and drove through, and we made it on home.

My trusty Alpine I

Alpine II

The Alpine II was easier to drive and an easier ride. I did a lot of freighting with this machine, hauling lumber and fuel. Bill Sr. is helping me on these freight loads. We made a pit stop at the Scary Tree, and the trail was great. Nice and smooth with no overflow today. Beautiful sunshine and a wonderful day, spending time with my son Bill.

INTERESTING LOADS

On the river again, hauling for my friends. The trails are great. Just some more interesting loads and another sunny day. These loads went up the Deshka River to about Mile 14. The tractor is ready to go, and in the second photo, we are jacking up the building to get the sleds under it.

THE LITTLE MAN ON MY SHOULDER

I had a gas run to Mile 18 on the Deshka River. When I got to a steep hill, the little man on my shoulder told me to unhook one sled. I did not listen to the advice; instead, I hit the gas and went for it. The back sled slid off the hill, and the front of my snowmachine went up and over on the left side, slamming me to the ground on the hard-packed snow trail. My left foot was stuck under the snowmachine, and I could feel that I had broken a rib.

I had to pull my foot out of my boot to get my foot unstuck. That took me fifteen minutes or more to get it free. I was now with one boot off and one boot on. I managed to get up, and I used my winch to pull my snowmachine upright. I found my other boot and put it on. I had to unhook both sleds and take them up the hill one at a time. I got both sleds hooked up again, but when I tried to take off, I spun out. I said a few choice words, spinning out every time I tried to take off.

The man who lived at Mile 18 and a neighbor of his came out to look for me, since I was overdue. We hooked up the three snowmachines, and together we pulled the sleds to a packed trail. The guys then hooked the sleds to their machines and took them on up to Mile 18. I turned around and headed home.

When I got home, I was colder than hell. Lucille had hot soup made, but when I tried to eat, I was shaking so hard I could not hold my spoon. I finally got warmed up enough to eat.

Always listen to the little man on your shoulder, because he will guide you right. It took me a long time to listen to him.

SAFER TO CRAWL

I had helped a friend haul some lumber to his cabin and was on my way back home on the snowmachine trail when I hit a bump really hard. The snowmachine came down so hard, it made a hole in my radiator. The antifreeze leaked out, and the hazard buzzer and red light came on. I saw an open lead a few feet from the trail, close enough that I decided not to walk over to it. It would be safer to crawl, so I got a can out of my pack and nervously crawled over to the open lead. I dipped some water out to put in the radiator, and then I drove a little farther and had to put more water in. I finally got to the Yentna Station, where I had a great cup of coffee and a hamburger.

Dan, the owner, told me to use his Bearcat to go the rest of the way, so I loaded my snowmachine onto my sled and came on home. Later I had a friend take the Bearcat back to the Yentna Station. (Thank you, Dan).

Folks always help along the river. No one wants to be stranded out in -20°F, or even sometimes -30°F temperatures. Friends, and even strangers, always help one another when there is trouble.

PTARMIGAN VALLEY

In the 1970s before we bought our land on the Yentna, we were living in the Chugiak area. We all had great times riding snowmachines in Ptarmigan Valley. A little too much whiskey, at times, for my brother Dale and me and other adults, and lots of snowmachine wrecks. We'd fix the snowmachines throughout the week and tear them up on weekends—at least they were beaters.

Billy had learned to ski, so I would pull him up the big hill, and Billy would ski back down. One evening when we were playing in Ptarmigan Valley, I decided I could ski. Billy pulled me and Jim Beam up the hill, then I started down on skis. Wasn't long until I fell and went the rest of the way down the hill head over heels. That's when I decided that I could not ski.

Another time Lucille and I were sitting on her snowmachine that wouldn't start. I was trying to start it, giving several pulls, but it still wasn't starting. I said something that she did not hear, so she leaned her head over to ask me what I said. About that time, I gave the snowmachine rope a good pull, my elbow smacked Lucille in the face, and she went flying off the machine. A friend was standing by and said, "Why did you do that? She didn't do anything." Lucille said she learned a lesson not to stick her head around when I'm pulling on a rope. She had a black eye for a long, long time.

A few weeks later, on a weekend, we were once again at our playground in Ptarmigan Valley. The kids and Lucille said they were getting cold and decided to go home. After a little whiskey for Dale and me, we decided we could go over another hill and a valley and come out in Eagle River, which we did. We rode down the road and stopped at Tips Bar for a few shots and then left. We decided we would ride down the Old Glenn Highway back to Chugiak.

Dale was riding in front, and I was following. The road was icy and slick. I hit a chunk of ice, which threw me off my machine. The machine kept running down the road and so did I, sliding on my ass down the road. I passed Dale. He caught up with me and got my machine stopped. Of course, we got it all together and came on home. For me, it was another cracked rib.

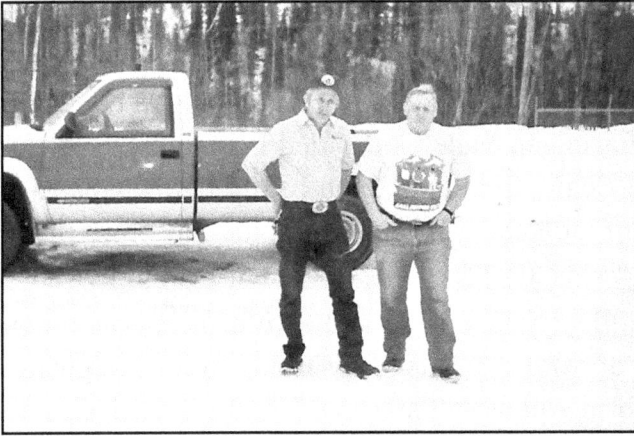

*Me and my brother Dale. We kinda grew up
and stopped doing crazy things.*

Rabbit Lake

Here it is March 2015, and we've had the lowest amount of snowfall since keeping records. I heard it during the weather on a local TV station, so I guess it's true. The snow is getting soft, and the river has a lot of ice patches. I was hauling a log splitter on my snowmachine to Rabbit Lake for Charlie, the Bear Man.

I was riding along just fine, thinking that this would be an easy haul. It had been a few years since I'd been to Rabbit Lake, and I was a few years older. I got up to the area and began wandering around, trying to find the lake. I began to come around, finding my own tracks, so I called a friend to see if he could tell me exactly where the turn off was, or if there were any sort of trail markings. He didn't really know.

I heard an airplane and looked up. The plane was circling and dipping his wings at the same place about three times. I realized it was Kenny Hughes in the plane, and I began to remember the airplane signals I had learned when I was taking flying lessons. I knew I was almost to the lake, and that was the signal Kenny was giving me.

I found the lake, and Kenny flew on, both of us happy. I unloaded the wood splitter and visited with Charlie for a while. Charlie was an interesting man who loved and photographed the bears that came to his property.

By the time I got home, the story was that Old Man River had gotten lost. I told them I wasn't lost—the cabin was. Hard to get lost, if a person keeps Sleeping Lady to his right.

Kenny Hughes is a great man who is always ready to help anyone in need. Kenny made sure everyone had a turkey for their Thanksgiving dinners. The river was not usually frozen enough for snowmachines to travel on in November, so he would drop frozen turkeys to the folks on the Yentna River from his airplane, and that's how he got known as the Turkey Bomber.

A few of the bears over the years at Charlie's place
(Images courtesy of Charlie, the Bear Man)

(Images courtesy of Charlie, the Bear Man)

PIZZAS

We built the Rebel Roost into a profitable lodge, and in 1997 we sold it to a couple that was famous for their fresh homemade pizzas. The day I hauled their Jeep up the Yentna for them, I had a pizza, and I can tell you that a person won't go away hungry—it was a huge pizza. The lodge was doing really well with lots of pizzas being made and sold, along with good, cold beer.

The next winter they called me to haul the Jeep back out to be repaired. And I had another great pizza.

SNOWY NIGHT

The winters have long nights with just a few hours of daylight to haul. I am usually still on the river at dark, and that is when I see the best northern lights. Sometimes there will be a beautiful full moon that gives me light, and at times it's just very dark. And sometimes it's snowing so much that I can barely see the trail.

I was on the trail one night when it was snowing huge, wet snowflakes that stuck to everything. I stopped at the Yentna Station for coffee, and as I was about to go in the door, Jennie (the co-owner) said, "Don't move, I want to take a picture." And this is the photo.

This is my first granddaughter, Amie. She was caught in a storm at a job site. Amie spent many weekends and summers with us as a young girl. Now she's all grown up.

Loading Sleds

We are getting the sleds loaded up for another river trip. My grandson Billy Jr. is helping me on these loads. He is visiting us on weekends and loves helping me haul. Back to school for him on Monday.

ANOTHER LOAD AND GRANDKIDS

I take the barrels in full and bring them back empty.
Another great freight run.

Every one of our grandkids grew up riding in this sled

Grandkids Carisa and Billy Jr. weekend at our house.
Ready to help load and always ready to ride.

I Love My Job

Freight going up the Yentna River to folks who are getting ready to build their getaway weekend cabins.

HAULING WHEELS

A friend of mine, Duane, has a cabin up the Deshka River. He asked if I could haul this pickup to his cabin. I like a challenge, so I told him I would do it. The trails were in great shape. I put the pickup on one of my Swiss-made sleds, hooked the sled up to my new Skandic super-wide snowmachine, and down the trail I went. It was a great trip, beautiful weather. Got the truck up to his place, and he asked if I would haul this Volkswagen back to the Deshka Landing. I did and had no problems at all.

TRAIL MARKERS

Why should you never knock down snowmachine trail markers? You just might be the next one in the hole.

In February 2007, I was pulling unloaded double sleds in from Lake Creek. It was a very dark night, and little did I know that up in front of me was an eight-foot drop-off with jumbled ice below. Some dumb ass had taken the warning trail markers down.

I saw it too late and tried to miss it, but my snowmachine slid sideways, and that rolled the sleds over the steep side of the drop-off. I was sliding with my machine, and it rolled and landed on top of me. I knew I had broken my back. I lay there a few minutes, and somehow, I managed to get the snowmachine off me and got the sleds unhooked from the snowmachine.

I got on the machine and rode it over to Willie's house. He then came back to the sleds with me and helped me get the sleds out of the drop-off and hooked up to my snowmachine again. Willie wanted to call Lucille so she could get Life-Med (the air evacuation team) to come and pick me up. I told him not to call Lucille at all, and that I would call him when I got home.

Yentna Station was sixteen river-trail miles downriver. I knew I would stop and have coffee and get something to eat. I decided to leave my sleds at the Yentna Station. Dan said he would bring them out for me.

I got back on my snowmachine, and Dan wedged a huge pillow behind me for back support. He and Jennie also wanted to call Life-Med and Lucille. I asked them not to because I did not want her to worry, and I didn't need to be flown out. I just wanted to get my snowmachine home. It was thirty-two river-trail miles from the Yentna Station to our house at the Deshka Landing.

Yes, I was in pain, but I ignored it. When I got home, Lucille wanted me to go to the ER. I said no and went to bed.

I woke up in a lot pain the next morning, so I had Lucille drive me to the emergency room. I had three broken vertebrates and three broken ribs. The doctor gave me a back brace and some pain pills, as there wasn't anything else they could do.

Later the VA sent me to physical therapy. I went a few times and didn't think it was doing any good, so I took the rest of the winter off and did my own therapy.

So now you know why no one should remove an "X" from a trail marker.

GOOD TIME FOR HEALING

It was a good time for healing. The stars were lined up perfectly. I got a phone call from Dianna and Neal Sullivan to join them on a boat trip from Washington to Alaska, going through the Inland Passage.

I was still healing from my broken back and decided this would give me a chance to really rest and heal. I could watch the sun come up and go down and hopefully watch a big, round moon glistening on the waters each night, while looking at all the stars. During the day I could be watching dolphins and whales, sea birds and any other sea creatures. All this for a month.

Of course, I said yes. Lucille and I flew to Seattle where Dianna and Neal picked us up. We went to the Hood Canal boat harbor where the boat *Dinero* was waiting. *Dinero* means money in Spanish. I just know it is a beautiful boat.

Some folks who had already been partying into the evening met us on the dock and handed us a drink. We sat around for a while swapping stories.

Soon it was time to lay our heads down for a few hours of sleep. It had been a long day, and we unfolded our sleeping bags that would be our nightly task. We were met by two giant schnauzers, Doc and Lilly. As we put our sleeping bags on the fold-out couch, Doc looked at us as if to say, "All right, a full bed tonight." Lilly stays with Dianna at night, and Doc always sleeps on the couch. He grumbled every night as we pulled him off the couch. Sometimes he was an amusing dog.

We were a few days into our trip when one evening, safely tucked in a cove, Neal put the shrimp pot down in the water, hopeful of bringing up some shrimp for a nice dinner. On this night he only brought up jellyfish. Neal laid the jelly fish on the back of the boat, and we were all looking at them before putting them back in water. We didn't notice that Doc, being the nosey dog that he was, put his nose and tongue on the jellyfish. Soon his nose began to itch bad, and he threw up. He ate lots of ice and tried to eat the throw rug. He was all over the floor scooting and rolling and pushing his nose and mouth on everything. I felt so sorry for him. Lucille kept rubbing his mouth with ice. Doc was entertaining us again. Finally, the sting went away. I doubt that it taught him a lesson. Doc was always ready for attention; Lily was shy and quiet and always stayed by Dianna's side.

The month-long trip on the *Dinero* was exciting. It was an awesome trip that we will always remember. We spent nights docked in beautiful coves and days on the water, sometimes rough water, sometimes smooth.

Our Captain Dianna and Mate Neal were very knowledge-able with the boat. We felt very safe and secure. I was feeling a lot better with the rest I was getting and the great days on the *Dinero*. I would be ready for my rivers when I returned home.

The Dinero

Our Captain Diana and Mate Neal

WILDLIFE WATCHING

I have always loved and admired wild animals. Some are a source of food, if needed, but we usually just watch them. The moose come in our yard every fall. One year I watched a mama moose get in Lucille's garden and eat the cabbage and broccoli and everything that was good. The babies ran around and around the garden fence, wondering how mama got in. I watched her jump back over and eat rose hips off the wild rose bushes, teaching her little ones.

We had two brown bear cubs in our yard one year. Mama must have been close by, but we never saw her. We had to take a picture before we told them to leave. They went running, and we could hear them running down the gravel road. We named them Flip and Flop, but they never returned.

Another year when our daughter Mitzi was visiting, she washed some clothes and hung them on the clothesline to dry. A little black bear came in the yard and pulled a shirt off the clothesline, sat down, and rubbed it all over his face and body. I guess it was attracted to the Downy scent. Mitzi ran out, yelling to him, "That's my favorite shirt! Why couldn't you get something else?" The bear took off, leaving Mitzi's shirt full of bear-claw holes.

One winter we even had a little fox that came into our yard and stayed for quite a while. We'd look out the window, and he'd be sitting on the porch step. I guess he felt safe around us. We have enjoyed living around and observing all the wildlife in the area throughout the years.

BABY FOXES

One year four kits were born in one of the culverts under a driveway. They would eventually wander out into the neighborhood, and it was very interesting watching them grow. When they grew up, they found other trails and moved on.

PORCUPINE

The other day I saw a porcupine crossing the road, and it made me remember Lucille telling me about the time our dog, Scrapper, and Billy's dog, Roach, got swiped by a porcupine. Our daughter-in-law, Cindy, and the grandkids were visiting me at the time. The dogs were out running in the woods, and when they came home, Roach had quills all over his face, inside his mouth, and around his eyes. Scrapper had only a few on his face, which were pulled out. Roach had a hundred or more; his face looked as if he had a white beard. He was running around and around the house, rubbing his face on the ground and foaming at the mouth. Lucille said she thought she would have to put him down because they could not hold him still to pull the quills out.

She called our Moose Creek neighbor, Ray, explained the situation, and asked if he would help. As usual, he was ready to help. Before long, she saw Ray coming down the river in his canoe, pipe in his mouth, and a smile on his face.

Ray began to come up with ideas: first he cut a hole in a large sock to go over Roach's body and put it on the dog with just his head sticking out. That still would not keep him from moving, though, so then they duct-taped his feet. He still moved too much to let them remove the quills.

Lucille called a veterinarian. He asked her if she had any type of medication to calm him down. She did have some Valium, so the veterinarian asked the dog's weight and strength of the pills. He told her to give Roach about four Valium, let him quiet down, and then pull the quills. Ray put the pills in a piece of hamburger and managed to get it down the dog's throat.

When Roach began to calm down, Ray and Cindy pulled quills for at least two hours, getting every quill out. Finally finished, Roach lay down and rested. He must have been so relieved and tired. They took the duct tape off his feet, since he wanted to come in the house. Roach gets up to walk up the steps and falls sideways, staggering like a real drunk person. They helped him in the house so he could sleep and rest. Scrapper lay down by Roach and looked at him as if to say, "I'm sorry, buddy."

Ray said he sure hoped the dogs learned a lesson. He had cup of coffee, and then he went on home. Lucille said she was so thankful for our good neighbors on Moose Creek.

Billy's dog Roach, feeling much better

Our dog Scrapper at the beginning of freeze up

MORE ENTERTAINMENT

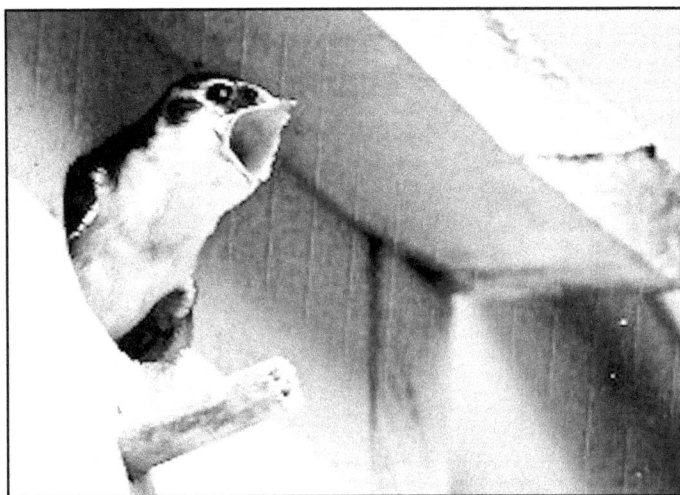

Owl and Chickadee, Squirrels, Butterfly, and More

I was coming in the house one day when I happened to look toward our wooded area and saw this owl with a chickadee sitting right along beside it. Lucille grabbed her camera and captured the moment. It is a northern saw-whet owl, and it's very unusual for a chickadee to be so close to an owl.

Alaska Moose

A moose is a curious animal and can be decoyed by a hunter, if he is skillful at imitating the moose call. I hope no hunter would be so lucky to get this moose. We called this moose Spike. One year he arrived at our lodge and just hung around. Spike would play with our dog, Scrapper. They would run around the yard playing with each other. Spike would eat the bird seed and bread scraps off our bird feeder. I guess we were his adopted parents. He would go off into the woods during the day to find and eat willow, then come back to us in the evening to sleep under our bedroom window.

Spike had a very strange hoofprint on one foot. If I saw his hoofprint in the snow, I knew he was somewhere around, even when I couldn't see him. I would yell, "Spike!" and he would come down off the hill or from across our spring flow. This was a year of very deep snow, so I cut wood, and Spike would clean up the brush. After the second winter he did not hang around, because he was big enough to take care of himself. I would occasionally see his hoofprint in the snow, then I knew he had been around. Lucille got brave enough to feed him from her hand. She said, "I still don't trust any moose—not even Spike." I only got this one photo of Lucille feeding him.

I love to watch moose in the yard

DEAD END EXPRESS

A National Geographic television series, Dead End Express, *was being filmed on the river a few years ago. Roger Phillips from Skwentna, Alaska, was the star. He wrote this story about his experience with the* Dead End Express *and his friendship with Larry.*

I moved to Alaska early in 2010 from northwest Ohio. I had no off-grid living experience and was a real cheechako (rookie Alaskan) when I got here. I had no idea what I was getting into, even though I thought I did. My wife and I bought a place 57 trail miles from the nearest road. No roads, no utilities. Totally off-grid with generator and solar power, and satellite communications with limited cell phone service. We live here full time, year-round.

I have to thank a couple of people for helping me out. The first one to show me anything about hauling freight with a snowmachine was Adam Gabryzak. The second person I must thank is Larry Heater. That old dude taught me things most people never get a chance to learn, let alone experience. Larry's love of the river, whether it was water or ice, was infectious. His eyes sparkled when he talked about barging or snow freighting. His stories never ended, and they always had a lesson embedded in them. Some were good lessons, and some were lessons of what not to do!

I had the pleasure of working with Larry for about nine years. He became a special part of my life. I will always treasure his friendship.

The best lesson Larry ever taught me was embedded in one of his stories when we were talking about one of my many freighting mishaps. Once I told him what I had done and how I had messed up, he looked at me with his sparkle and a smile and said, "You didn't listen to the little man, did ya?"

Of course, I had to ask, "What little man?"

Then his stories began about several mishaps he'd had. At the conclusion of his stories, Larry said, "Ya know, every time I had one of those things happen, there was a little voice in my head that said, 'You shouldn't, or something's not right.'" He continued, "I used to argue with that voice in my head and overrule that voice. Almost every time I did, I got into trouble. I finally named that voice the little man. We all have that little man in our head that knows better than we do. You just need to learn to listen to him and quit arguing." The little man in my head now has Larry's voice! I still hear ya, buddy.

In 2015, I got to participate in making a show for the National Geographic Channel called *Dead End Express*. The show was about various people and methods of hauling freight to remote locations (supposedly a dead end). I was featured in 88 minutes of airtime over four episodes of the show. I was the only snowmachine freighter on the show. Of course, I only knew how to do this because of the folks mentioned earlier.

I almost always had the materials I was to haul delivered to Larry and Lucille's property where Larry would help me load my freight and share a story. After about four or five times of going to Larry's with the film crew, I showed up one day without them. Larry looked at me, smiled, and said, "Where are your ducks?"

"Ducks?" I asked.

"Yeah, your ducks that are always following you around. You remind me of a mother duck keeping all of your ducklings in a row." And so, the film crew became known as the ducklings. Imagine, five guys, none with much snowmachine experience, following me around up to 120 miles of trails (one way) in remote Alaska and having no idea where they were. No roads, not many services, and rarely even a cell phone signal. Yep, I had a flock of ducklings.

These guys fell in love with Larry and his stories as well. They asked him many times to participate more in the show. He refused, only allowing them to take a few cameo shots of him. Some of the best pictures I have seen of him, came from those guys.

We had great laughs while they learned bush lessons, made mistakes and retakes. They never asked me to make stuff up or to purposely get myself into trouble. We did reenact of one of my previous mistakes that I had told them about. I thought I could do it safely this time. Nope, I jumped over an ice shelf with my machine and empty freight sleds. The sleds hooked the shelf and literally blew apart. It cost me a few bruises and a few hundred dollars to fix the sleds. They didn't ask me to do anymore dumb stuff. That shot did make the opener of the show, though!

As the filming continued, I had a couple of snowmachine failures that they caught on film and got stuck a few times in deep snow, but I didn't have any of the big drama stuff they were really hoping for. Ya see, I had already learned to listen to my little man.

We got to introduce some bush dwellers and share their stories, and we got to film some beautiful scenery. The show lasted one season here in the United States and is still airing in different countries all over the world. I still receive Facebook friend requests from all over the world due to the show. No, I don't accept them. I live in the bush of Alaska for a reason. I like to choose my friends and am very fortunate to have guys like Larry choose me as their friend.

THANK-YOU NOTES

These are just a few of the many, many thank-you notes that I've received over the years. I want to thank everyone for putting your trust in my hobby. I love the river, and it is a blessing that I've been able to be on it year after year, in both winter and summer, just doing what I love.

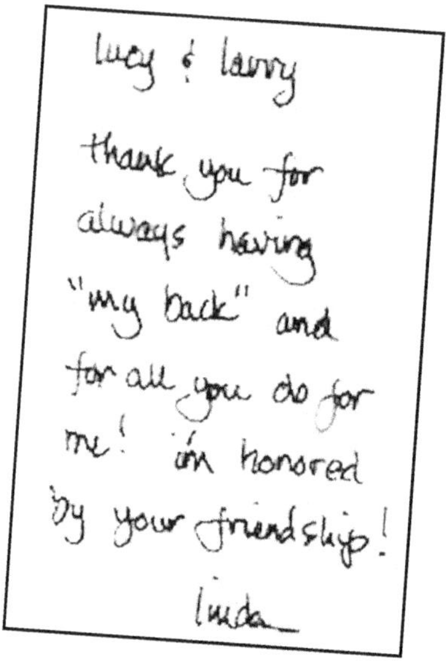

Lucy & Larry

thank you for always having "my back" and for all you do for me! I'm honored by your friendship!

Linda

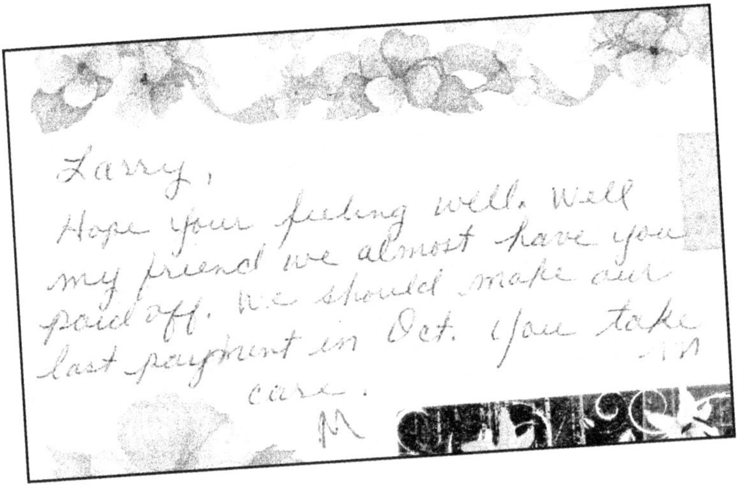

Larry,
Hope your feeling well. Well my friend we almost have you paid off. We should make our last payment in Oct. You take care.
M

LARRY:
Thank you For All The
Help in getting My
Ties To The Cabin ...
Couldn't Do it without
You ...

Thanks AGAIN

WALT

Larry & Lucille –
Thanks Ever so much
For All your help & Friendship
over the course of All these
years. Hope you Enjoy this MOOSE
Book As much As we have. They certainly have
A place on God's green Earth ... Right Next
To the potatoes' And GRAVEY!!

Merry Xmass
Mike & Mart
2011

115

HARRY & LUCILLE,
SETSUKO & I FEEL BLESSED TO HAVE QUALITY FRIENDS LIKE YOU. WE WISH YOU CONTINUED HAPPINESS AND GOOD HEATH DURING THIS HOLY SEASON.

Roy & SETSUKO

"In him was life; and the life was the light of men."   John 1:4

9-7-

LARRY,
THANKS FOR THE BOAT TOW

DALE

Dear Larry
Thanks for transporting our 4-wheeler
much appreciated –
you're the best!!

See ya on the River,
Bryan & Teresa

P.S. Happy Birthday

116

Thanks for
all the Help
and Support!

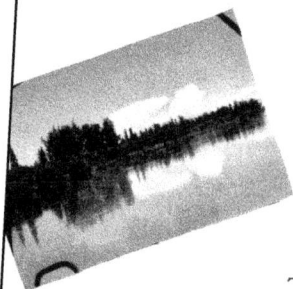

THANK YOU   09-08-09

Hi Larry!
    Thank you so much! For Picking
us up @ Seal beach! It took away
the big concern I had with hauling
the Widgen Motors up the Big-Sur!
I am so glad you are out here on the

River helping People with their
River Needs. Your face was a welcome
site for me and Marjorie! I hope
In the future to be building up on my
Property on the Hewit and will definitly
Need your services there! Thank again
                        Carter & Marjorie

117

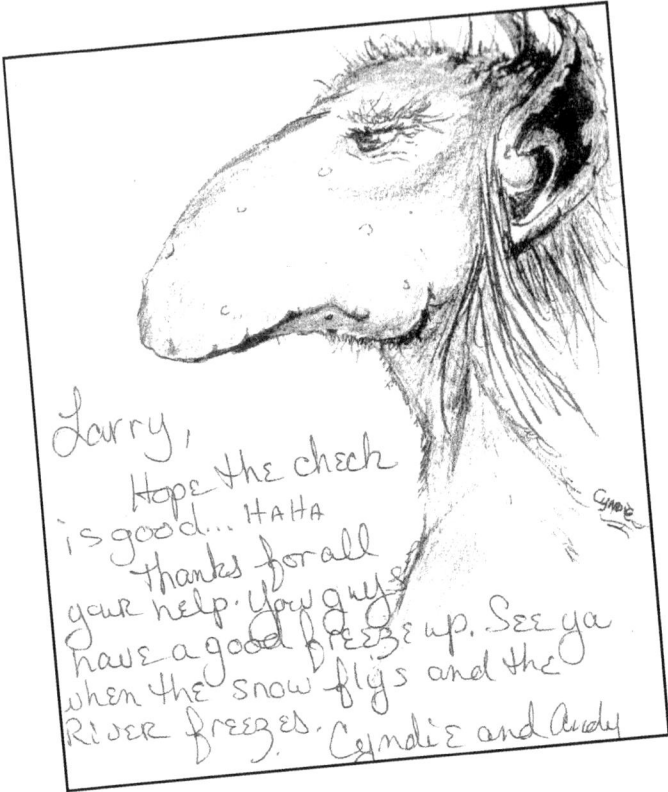

Larry,
    Hope the check
is good... HAHA
    thanks for all
your help. You guys
have a good FREEZE up. See ya
when the snow flies and the
RIVER freezes. Cyndie and Andy

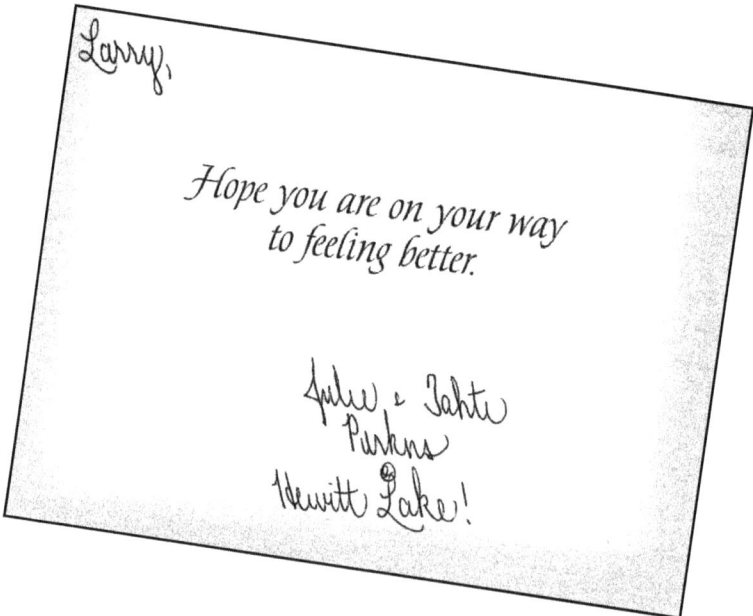

Larry,

*Hope you are on your way
to feeling better.*

Julie & Jahte
Purkins
Hewitt Lake!

P.S. Thanks for all you do for Aren. It means a lot to us – and him too, even tho he might not say so. He thinks you're the BOMB – I guess that means the best.

Susan and Eric

THANKS A HEAP! (with the Boat!)

David & Valerie Raatz

Larry & Lucille Heater

Thank you for being there when we needed you.

T. Goso

Thanks Larry —

Really Appreciate

Your Help

Walt

P.S. Stay Healthy — HANA

MANY MOONS

Many moons have passed since my Alaska or Bust dream came true. Ending up where I am today, life could not be any better. I will keep running the Susitna and the Yentna Rivers until I take my last breath.

Afterword

Take me to the river.

Rest in Peace

Larry Heater

1937–2019

TRIBUTES FROM FAMILY

MY GRANDFATHER

So, as some of you know, today a memorial service was held for my grandfather, Larry Heater. Over a hundred people showed up to pay their respects to him. I'm willing to bet that is not even a quarter of the people whose lives he has touched and changed through his actions. He was a man among men, a husband, a father, an uncle, a grandfather, a friend, a soldier, a hard worker, a fighter, a hero. But the only word I can think to fully describe my grandfather is a legend. He was a living legend that many had the pleasure to meet, and I am honored to be his grandson. He did the work of three men in his later years, if that tells you how great a man he really was. He wasn't just strong physically with the endurance of a team of oxen but his personality, as well as his mental acuity were also strong.

He was a helping hand to take, a shoulder you could always lean on, a pillar of strength to not only his large family but to his friends and the entire river community. So, tonight I honor his memory in the best way a soldier can. Tonight, I raise a glass in my grandfather's name. To Larry Heater: May he be immortalized in our hearts and actions. I hope to be half the man he was.

Billy Jr.
March 30, 2019

MY POPS

My dad is a man like no other. He gave me a life I would have never had if it wasn't for my pops, Larry Heater. He taught me, fought for me, held me, shouted at me, kissed me, but most importantly, loved me unconditionally.

There are not enough words I can say to describe just how important my pops was to me. He taught me so much: to work hard, to respect our elders, and to rely on myself.

My pops may not have been my birth father, but he is the person who taught me just about everything I have done in my life. I love and miss you, Pops.

Your son,
Billy Sr.

FEARLESS LEADER

This letter from Larry's son, Richard Heater, was read at Larry's Celebration of Life on March 30, 2019.

All Hail the "Fearless Leader," Larry Heater!

Larry was a humble man with a huge personality. Loved and respected by his community and friends, but most of all, his family.

Dad touched many lives by his kind deeds and willingness to help those in need. He had perseverance and a stubborn attitude, but he was honest, loyal, had integrity with good morals, and a genuine spirit.

Whether it was handing you a *red-hot* spark plug with his calloused fingers, a surprise slug in the arm, or his five a.m. wake-up call via shotgun blast outside your bedroom window, Dad never lost his boyish sense of humor. Quick with a joke or one of his old-time adages, he always managed to squeeze a little fun out of everything he did.

Dad always "ran point" on his many adventures. If Larry was leading the way, you always knew you were going to make it through alive. I've heard many a person say that there's nobody they would rather be stuck in the woods with than Larry Heater. It seemed like Dad knew every lake, creek, river bend and shortcut on the river—not to mention every gravel bar and shallow spot—he had many bent props to prove it!

Many people gravitated towards Dad; he was just fun to be around. We once took a trip to an old gold mine. It was some kind of historic tourist attraction. He was standing there with his white beard, cap, clunky boots, and old blue jeans. The tourists started gathering around him because they thought he was one of the old miners or a costumed tour guide. In all fairness, he did look like an old sourdough. They started asking him questions to which he replied, "We used to run snowmachines up here." What he meant was that he used to ride snowmobiles there back in the day. The tourists thought he was a miner, and that he used to run some kind of mining equipment. I still get a kick out of that every time I think of it.

One time we were snowmobiling in the backcountry and came across an open patch of water. Dad said, "We gotta cross that!" I thought he had lost his mind.

In terror, I asked, "Why do we have to do that?"

He whipped around, looked me dead in the eye, and shouted, "For the adventure!" And away we went! That's how Dad lived life—with an unquenchable thirst for thrill and adventure.

Dad once said, "Boy, they're going to miss me when I'm gone." And he was right. You never realize how much you love someone till you can no longer tell them that you do. I will always miss you, and I will always love you, and I will always cherish our time together.

Your son,
Richard

POP

My pop was and always will be my hero. He was a mountain man and a river legend. He was the kindest and strongest man I have ever known. He also was the most honest, always helping me and total strangers. He was rough and strong and could fix anything. He looked tough, but he would smile and then you would see the kindness and the kid in him. He loved to play jokes on everyone and had a sense of humor if someone got him. He taught me about life and to be honest and hard working. The best pop in the world. My pop was my hero and a true Alaskan legend.

I miss and love you, Pop, forever and always.

Your daughter,
Mitzi

UNCLE LARRY

I will forever be grateful to have had this Alaskan legend in my life. My Uncle Larry and Aunt Lucille left for the Last Frontier in 1973 and built a new life, filled with adventures.

I spent my childhood visiting my Alaska family. Their first home didn't have running water, so everything was the old-fashioned way. I learned to ski on the backroads with my cousin, Billy, and snowmachine on the frozen lakes. I once broke Uncle Larry's ribs spinning donuts on Eklutna Lake. I learned to hunt rabbits with him, but I quickly learned that was not my thing.

Years later Uncle Larry and Aunt Lucille built the Rebel Roost. Everything had to be hauled in via boat, plane, or snow-mobile. Uncle Larry found his calling in freighting supplies, oil, building products and rescuing boaters. He never ever turned a call down. Television approached him for a reality series, which he adamantly rejected. He was a humble man.

They later moved to the Deshka Landing, where he was a fixture on the river with his boat, freighting nearly every day during the spring, summer, and fall. All winter, he was freighting on his snowmachine and sleds. I was grateful to go on some river runs with him the last two summers. We hauled building supplies and rescued some rafters who had been fishing. He knew every spot on that river. On one of our last rides, the steering went out on his boat, and we were very heavy with lumber. I thought for sure the boat would tip in the swift current, and I was ready to swim to shore if the boat toppled over. Somehow, he repaired it, and we were on our way again. As you can tell by his biceps, this man was in amazing shape. There was nothing he couldn't fix or do himself.

Last summer I stayed with Uncle Larry and Aunt Lucille while I was living my Alaskan aviation dream. He couldn't work as much, as his heart was failing. I needed a car to travel to various airports to work, and he was so happy to find me a little beater pickup in Talkeetna. We had a good time splitting wood when I last saw him. I was determined to make sure they had enough wood cut when I left, even though he swore he could do it all. And he really could do it all! Until the day his heart just quit.

I'll forever cherish the memories I had with this adventurous, inspiring uncle of mine.

Uncle Larry rode into the Alaskan sunset one last time.

Your niece,
Angela Krieg

LARRY AND ME

I loved him from the beginning and forever.
We were soulmates 1972–2019.

I wish he could have lived to read his book.
He would be proud.

To Order Books

Please contact the publisher to order a copy of
Yentna Old Man River: Larry Heater, Rescue Man
by Lucille Heater.

Northbooks

www.northbooks.com
orders@northbooks.com

www.ingramcontent.com/pod-product-compliance
Lightning Source LLC
Chambersburg PA
CBHW051718090426
42738CB00010B/1976